MW01058287

THIS JOURNAL
BELONGS TO

_____

A LITTLE GOD TIME

JOURNAL

FOR MOTHERS

BELLE CITY GIFTS

Belle City Gifts
Racine, Wisconsin, USA

Belle City Gifts is an imprint of BroadStreet Publishing Group LLC.
Broadstreetpublishing.com

A LITTLE **GOD** TIME ❁ MOTHERS Journal

© 2015 by BroadStreet Publishing

ISBN 978-1-4245-5148-4

Cover and interior image © Bigstock/lozas

Cover and interior design by Garborg Design Works | www.garborgdesign.com
Compiled and edited by Michelle Winger | www.literallyprecise.com

Printed in China.

15   16   17   18   19   20   21   7   6   5   4   3   2   1

INTRODUCTION

A little God time is what all mothers need but
can rarely find in the craziness of everyday life.

If you take just a few moments to sit and write,
while pondering the inspirational quotes and
Scripture found on each page of this journal, you
can find the grace and strength you need to get
through your day.

Be encouraged as you reflect on the blessing
of motherhood in the midst of all the hard work.
Know that every sacrifice you make does not go
unnoticed.

May joy and peace be yours as you endeavor to
love your children as the heavenly Father loves you.

"Therefore I tell you, do not worry about your life.... Can any one of you by worrying add a single hour to your life?"

MATTHEW 6:25, 27 NIV

_____

_____

_____

_____

_____

_____

_____

_____

_____

_____

_____

_____

_____

_____

_____

_____

_____

_____

_____

Of all the things God asks us to
let go of, for a mother, worry just
might be the most difficult.

A peaceful heart leads to a healthy body;
jealousy is like cancer in the bones.

PROVERBS 14:30 NLT

_____
_____
_____
_____
_____
_____
_____
_____
_____
_____
_____
_____
_____
_____
_____
_____
_____
_____
_____
_____
_____

There will always be someone else that
has more than we do. Choosing to be
content with where we are in life will
bring us peace.

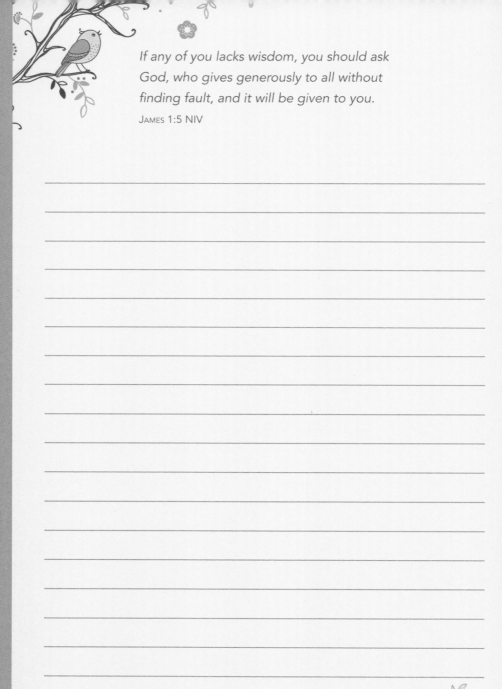

If any of you lacks wisdom, you should ask God, who gives generously to all without finding fault, and it will be given to you.

JAMES 1:5 NIV

_____

_____

_____

_____

_____

_____

_____

_____

_____

_____

_____

_____

_____

_____

_____

_____

_____

_____

_____

_____

_____

_____

A child is blessed to have a mother who
habitually goes to the feet of God to
petition for wisdom.

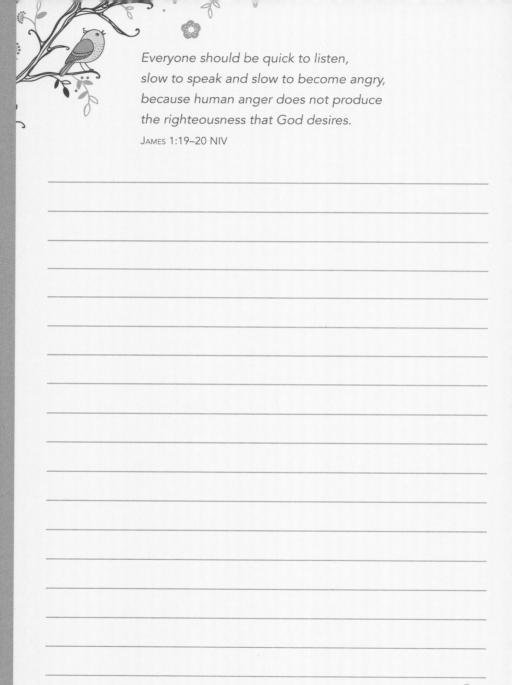

*Everyone should be quick to listen,
slow to speak and slow to become angry,
because human anger does not produce
the righteousness that God desires.*

JAMES 1:19–20 NIV

For being such adorable creatures, kids sure can
evoke a surprising amount of anger in us, can't they?

We will not hide these truths from our children;
we will tell the next generation
*about the glorious deeds of the L*ORD,
about his power and his mighty wonders.

PSALM 78:4 NLT

_____

_____

_____

_____

_____

_____

_____

_____

_____

_____

_____

_____

_____

_____

_____

_____

_____

_____

While they are growing in maturity of their faith, fight *for* your kids, not *against* them. Fight for them like God fights for you every day.

To everything there is a season,
A time for every purpose under heaven.

ECCLESIASTES 3:1 NKJV

Don't wish away those younger years of messes and diapers. Don't miss your current season by always looking to the next one. The gift of perspective knows that there are treasures in every season.

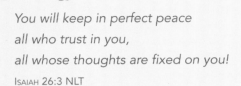

You will keep in perfect peace
all who trust in you,
all whose thoughts are fixed on you!
Isaiah 26:3 NLT

_____

_____

_____

_____

_____

_____

_____

_____

_____

_____

_____

_____

_____

_____

_____

_____

_____

_____

_____

Peace gives us the ability to stay strong
even when life is hard. Peace comforts
us when our world falls apart.

I have swept away your fences like a cloud,
your sins like the morning mist.
Return to me, for I have redeemed you.

Isaiah 44:22 NIV

_____

_____

_____

_____

_____

_____

_____

_____

_____

_____

_____

_____

_____

_____

_____

_____

_____

_____

_____

_____

_____

_____

If anything can reveal our flaws and mistakes,
motherhood can. It sheds light on our weaknesses
and keeps us humble. God uses our children to
unearth our shortcomings and encourage change.

"Don't let your hearts be troubled.
Trust in God, and trust also in me."

JOHN 14:1 NLT

_____

_____

_____

_____

_____

_____

_____

_____

_____

_____

_____

_____

_____

_____

_____

_____

_____

_____

We should purpose to live our lives with
complete trust in God. Our confidence
in him is a wonderful testimony to our
children of his faithfulness.

"The Lord your God is in your midst,
A victorious warrior.
He will exult over you with joy,
He will be quiet in His love,
He will rejoice over you with shouts of joy."
Zephaniah 3:17 NASB

Each day in our children's lives has value
and importance to the Father. To him,
every day is worth being celebrated.

You know that the testing of your faith produces perseverance.

JAMES 1:3 NIV

Our faith in God and our hope in him make
us unbreakable when presented with affliction.
Trials make us more aware of his work in our lives.

*The faithful love of the L*ORD *never ends!*
His mercies never cease.
Great is his faithfulness;
his mercies begin afresh each morning.

LAMENTATIONS 3:22-23 NLT

_____

_____

_____

_____

_____

_____

_____

_____

_____

_____

_____

_____

_____

_____

_____

_____

_____

We may have used up our allotment of
God's mercy yesterday, but there is new
mercy available for us today. He pours it
fresh into our hearts every morning.

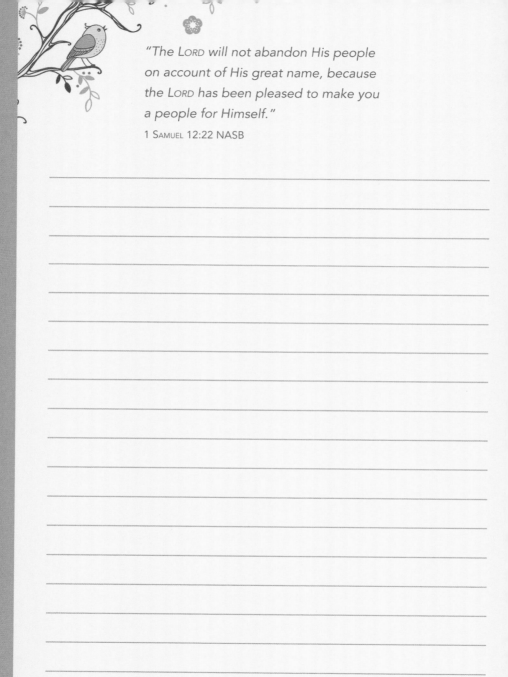

"The LORD will not abandon His people on account of His great name, because the LORD has been pleased to make you a people for Himself."

1 SAMUEL 12:22 NASB

_____

_____

_____

_____

_____

_____

_____

_____

_____

_____

_____

_____

_____

_____

_____

_____

_____

_____

_____

_____

Children aren't afraid to say when they
are frightened, confused, or worried. They
are expected to take these needs to their
parents and get direction and comfort.
We can do the same with God.

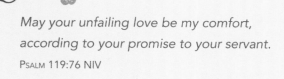

May your unfailing love be my comfort,
according to your promise to your servant.

PSALM 119:76 NIV

_____

_____

_____

_____

_____

_____

_____

_____

_____

_____

_____

_____

_____

_____

_____

_____

_____

_____

You will laugh again in the morning and
find peace even in your grief.

The day is yours, and yours also the night;
you established the sun and moon.
It was you who set all the boundaries of the earth;
you made both summer and winter.

Psalm 74:16-17 NIV

Winter treasures are like manna—the same
manna would be rotten in the summer.

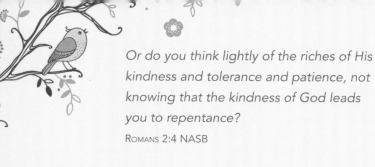

Or do you think lightly of the riches of His kindness and tolerance and patience, not knowing that the kindness of God leads you to repentance?

ROMANS 2:4 NASB

God knows a corrective word spoken in love
will produce more than a shouting match.
He knows it is his firm but gentle touch that
will bring about a heart change.

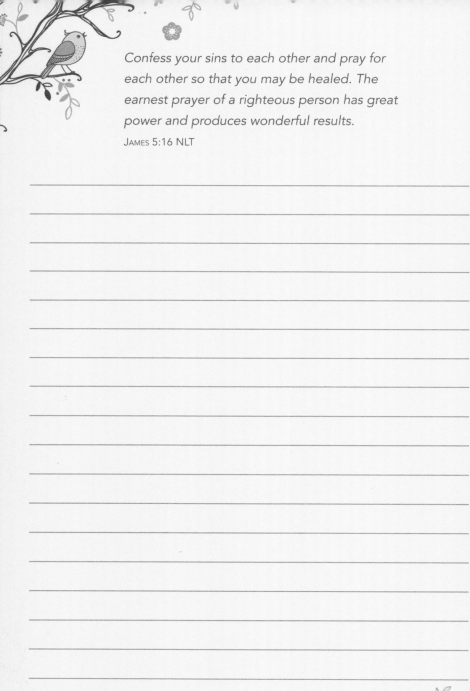

Confess your sins to each other and pray for each other so that you may be healed. The earnest prayer of a righteous person has great power and produces wonderful results.

JAMES 5:16 NLT

_____

_____

_____

_____

_____

_____

_____

_____

_____

_____

_____

_____

_____

_____

_____

_____

_____

_____

_____

_____

_____

_____

God wants us to support each other in the
messiest parts of our lives, and the only way
we can do that is by letting a friend in.

"The Lord disciplines those he loves, and he punishes each one he accepts as his child."

Hebrews 12:6 NLT

God disciplines us for our own good using the gentlest
means possible to provoke the greatest change.

He has told you, O man, what is good;
And what does the Lᴏʀᴅ require of you
But to do justice, to love kindness,
And to walk humbly with your God?

Mɪᴄᴀʜ 6:8 NASB

Your children don't need a perfect
mother—so it won't do them any
good pretending you are.

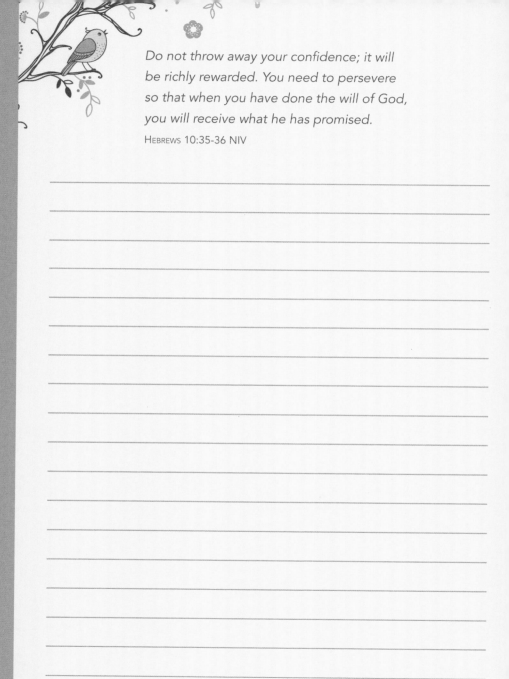

Do not throw away your confidence; it will be richly rewarded. You need to persevere so that when you have done the will of God, you will receive what he has promised.

HEBREWS 10:35-36 NIV

God is in your corner shouting praises of
encouragement in any and every situation!

"I am the true vine, and My Father is the vinedresser.
Every branch in Me that does not bear fruit,
He takes away; and every branch that bears fruit,
He prunes it so that it may bear more fruit."

JOHN 15:1-2 NASB

Pruning isn't for the sake of staying small.
It is so we can bear even more fruit.

"I am the resurrection and the life. The one who believes in me will live, even though they die; and whoever lives by believing in me will never die."

JOHN 11:25-26 NIV

Real insurance rests only in the promises of
God and our promise of salvation bought
by the blood of Jesus Christ.

As the Scriptures say, "If you want to boast, boast only about the LORD."
When people commend themselves, it doesn't count for much. The important thing is for the Lord to commend them.

2 CORINTHIANS 10:17-18 NLT

If our kids are wonderful—if we are
wonderful—it's because God wanted it so.

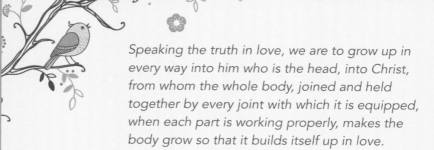

Speaking the truth in love, we are to grow up in every way into him who is the head, into Christ, from whom the whole body, joined and held together by every joint with which it is equipped, when each part is working properly, makes the body grow so that it builds itself up in love.

EPHESIANS 4:15-16 ESV

_____

_____

_____

_____

_____

_____

_____

_____

_____

_____

_____

_____

_____

_____

_____

_____

_____

_____

Friends are valuable. Mothering with the support of people that love and care for us is priceless. We need each other.

*The LORD is good to those who depend on him,
to those who search for him.
So it is good to wait quietly
for salvation from the LORD.*

LAMENTATIONS 3:25-26 NLT

Jesus spent a lot of time in relationship with others.
His *busy* was different than ours.

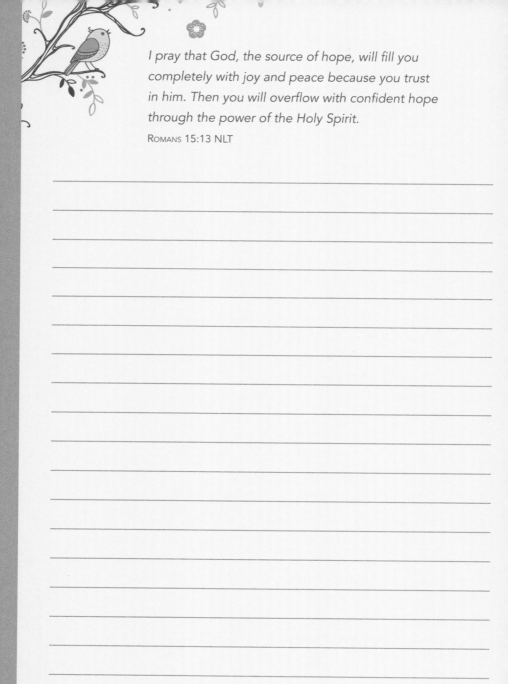

I pray that God, the source of hope, will fill you completely with joy and peace because you trust in him. Then you will overflow with confident hope through the power of the Holy Spirit.

ROMANS 15:13 NLT

Even if days of doubt come more often than not, be confident of this: God knew exactly what he was doing when he trusted you with your precious children—with *his* precious children.

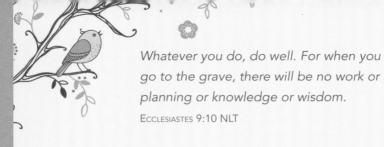

Whatever you do, do well. For when you go to the grave, there will be no work or planning or knowledge or wisdom.

Ecclesiastes 9:10 NLT

Every day you wake up is a new opportunity to
put everything you are into your work—whether
that work is inside your home or out.

You are my refuge and my shield;
your word is my source of hope.
PSALM 119:114 NLT

_____

_____

_____

_____

_____

_____

_____

_____

_____

_____

_____

_____

_____

_____

_____

_____

_____

_____

_____

_____

Next time motherhood overwhelms you,
hide away with God's Word (and perhaps
some well-deserved chocolate). He will give
you the rest you need.

"You are the light of the world. A town built on a hill cannot be hidden.... Let your light shine before others, that they may see your good deeds and glorify your Father in heaven."

MATTHEW 5:14,16 NIV

Being a role model is a huge responsibility, and the
scary thing is, you are one—all the time—whether
you want to be or not.

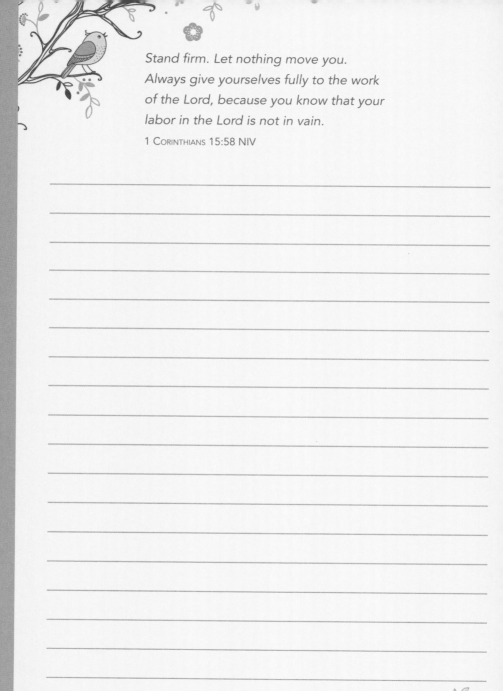

Stand firm. Let nothing move you.
Always give yourselves fully to the work
of the Lord, because you know that your
labor in the Lord is not in vain.

1 CORINTHIANS 15:58 NIV

When you are confident of what God's will
is, choose to stay firm in your decisions even
when your children, or others, plead with you to
change your mind.

"Be still, and know that I am God.
I will be exalted among the nations,
I will be exalted in the earth!"

PSALM 46:10 ESV

_____

_____

_____

_____

_____

_____

_____

_____

_____

_____

_____

_____

_____

_____

_____

_____

_____

_____

_____

_____

_____

_____

In the rush and busyness of motherhood, God
has not left you alone. He wants to give you rest
and encouragement.

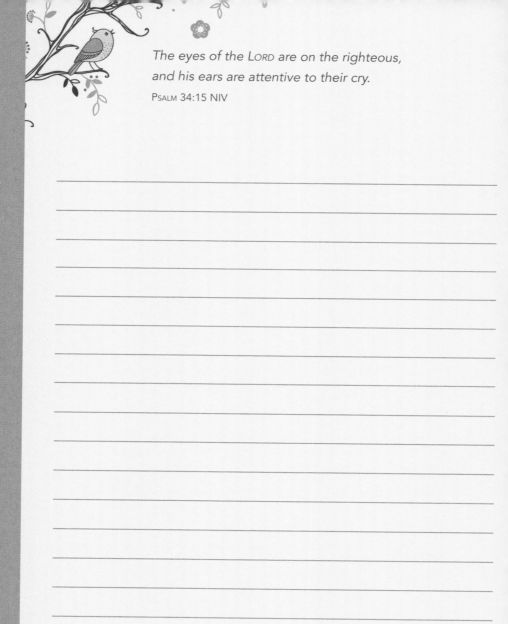

*The eyes of the L*ORD *are on the righteous,*
and his ears are attentive to their cry.

PSALM 34:15 NIV

Do you know in the depths of your heart that
your prayers are heard: both the shouting
cries for help and the gentle whispers of
thanksgiving? They are.

They who wait for the LORD shall renew their strength;
they shall mount up with wings like eagles;
they shall run and not be weary;
they shall walk and not faint.

ISAIAH 40:31 ESV

God does not ask you to wait for him because
he is too busy. He knows there is joy for you in
anticipating what is to come.

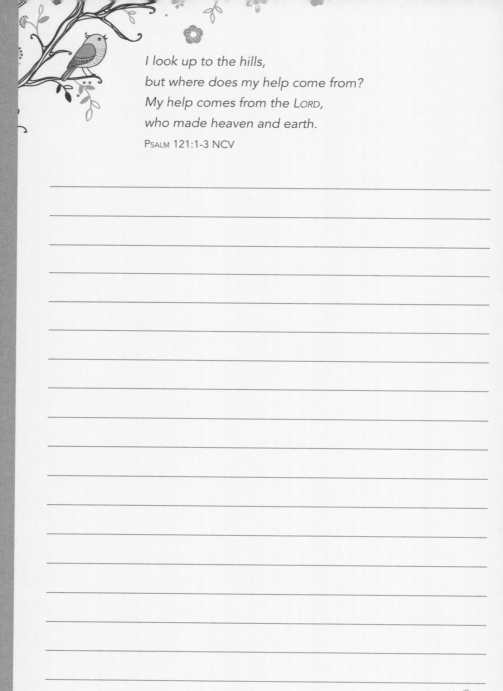

I look up to the hills,
but where does my help come from?
My help comes from the LORD,
who made heaven and earth.
PSALM 121:1-3 NCV

God asks you to take a chance on the people he's intricately placed in your life. You'll be amazed at how much stronger you feel when you're leaning on those who want to carry the load with you.

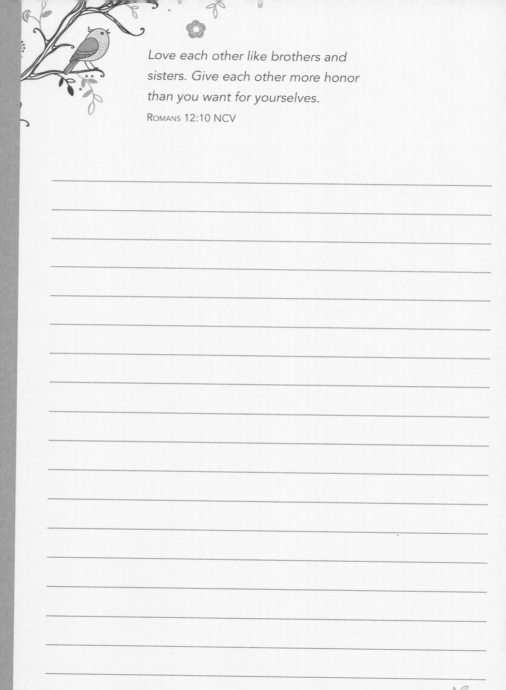

Love each other like brothers and sisters. Give each other more honor than you want for yourselves.

ROMANS 12:10 NCV

_____

_____

_____

_____

_____

_____

_____

_____

_____

_____

_____

_____

_____

_____

_____

_____

_____

_____

_____

_____

Small acts of kindness can be deeply impacting.
You never know how encouraging a simple act of
kindness can be to another mom.

A generous person will prosper;
whoever refreshes others will be refreshed.

PROVERBS 11:25 NIV

God uses strangers, neighbors, friends, family, and
even our children to convey his message of truth.
He bestows wisdom to us in all forms.
Usually these messages come as a breath
of fresh air at just the time we need them.

I am my beloved's,
And his desire is toward me.

Song of Solomon 7:10 NKJV

Nothing is strong enough to separate us
from God's love. It still wins hearts.
It still conquers self-doubt and hatred.
It silences our accusers. It says,
"This is my bride, and I love her!"

Love never gives up, never loses faith, is always hopeful, and endures through every circumstance.

1 Corinthians 13:7 NLT

Show your children more grace by loving them
unconditionally. Let them be found saying,
"It's okay; I made a mistake, but I'm still loved."

"Give, and it will be given to you. A good measure, pressed down, shaken together and running over, will be poured into your lap. For with the measure you use, it will be measured to you."

LUKE 6:38 NIV

The world may see you as "just a mom," but in God's eyes, your job is important. Raising children to be tenderhearted toward God is one of the greatest tasks you can be called to.

Love keeps no record of wrongs

1 CORINTHIANS 13:5 NIV

_____

_____

_____

_____

_____

_____

_____

_____

_____

_____

_____

_____

_____

_____

_____

_____

_____

_____

_____

_____

_____

_____

_____

_____

_____

_____

_____

_____

_____

_____

_____

_____

_____

_____

_____

_____

_____

_____

True love releases past mistakes and
genuinely believes for the best next time.

"Humanly speaking, it is impossible.
But with God everything is possible."

MATTHEW 19:26 NLT

Jesus couldn't say it enough, and you can't hear it enough. You will never please God, and never enter his kingdom, on your own power.

"If you keep my commandments, you will abide in my love, just as I have kept my Father's commandments and abide in his love. These things I have spoken to you, that my joy may be in you, and that your joy may be full."

JOHN 15:10-11 ESV

_____

_____

_____

_____

_____

_____

_____

_____

_____

_____

_____

_____

_____

_____

_____

_____

_____

_____

We are much more productive and joyful
when we spend time in God's presence.

"If I then, your Lord and Teacher, have washed your feet, you also ought to wash one another's feet."

JOHN 13:14 NKJV

We serve our families because we love them, but it's easy to forget that day after day with our hands in dirty dishwater. In those times, we need to remember Jesus, who humbly knelt before his disciples to wash their feet.

"Whoever exalts himself will be humbled,
and whoever humbles himself will be exalted."

Matthew 23:12 ESV

_____

_____

_____

_____

_____

_____

_____

_____

_____

_____

_____

_____

_____

_____

_____

_____

_____

_____

_____

_____

God wants us to know that he sees us. Every sleepless
night, the burn in our muscles from holding our
babies, and the monotony of daily chores have not
gone unnoticed by him. He sees it all.

If our hearts condemn us, we know that God is greater than our hearts, and he knows everything.

1 JOHN 3:20

Have you become your own worst critic? Instead of judging your every thought and action, spend time in his presence and hear his sacred message for you—you are loved, adored, and precious in his sight.

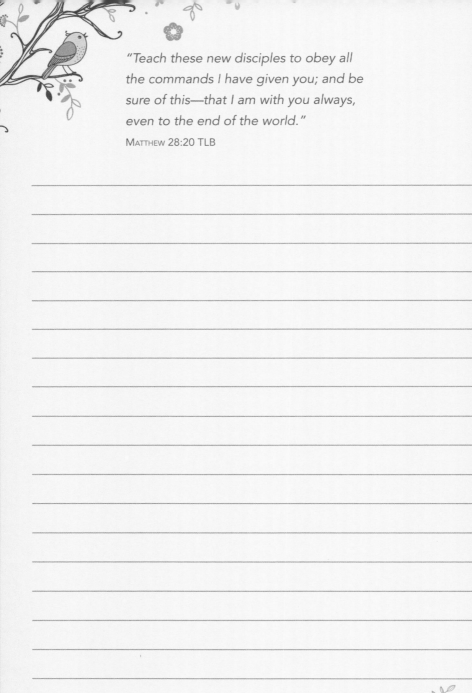

"Teach these new disciples to obey all
the commands I have given you; and be
sure of this—that I am with you always,
even to the end of the world."

Matthew 28:20 TLB

Circumstances don't matter as much
when God is with us.

He makes me lie down in green pastures;
He leads me beside quiet waters.
He restores my soul.

PSALM 23:2-3 NASB

There are times that you might feel like you are going
crazy from all the noise around you. On those days,
let God lead you to quiet waters.

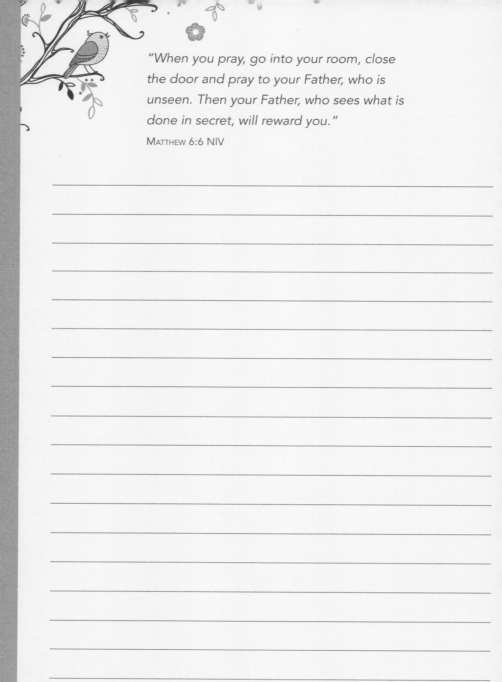

"When you pray, go into your room, close the door and pray to your Father, who is unseen. Then your Father, who sees what is done in secret, will reward you."

MATTHEW 6:6 NIV

_____

_____

_____

_____

_____

_____

_____

_____

_____

_____

_____

_____

_____

_____

_____

_____

_____

_____

_____

_____

Can you get away today in secret to pray?
In secret, God will reward your heart. Make
sneaking away with him a daily routine.

"Come," my heart says, "seek his face!"
Your face, LORD, do I seek.
Do not hide your face from me.

PSALM 27:8-9 NRSV

_____

_____

_____

_____

_____

_____

_____

_____

_____

_____

_____

_____

_____

_____

_____

_____

_____

_____

_____

_____

Do you wonder how God's face appears when he looks at you? Be assured, his eyes are more gentle than you expect. His expression is more tender than you thought. His posture is more approachable than you perceived.

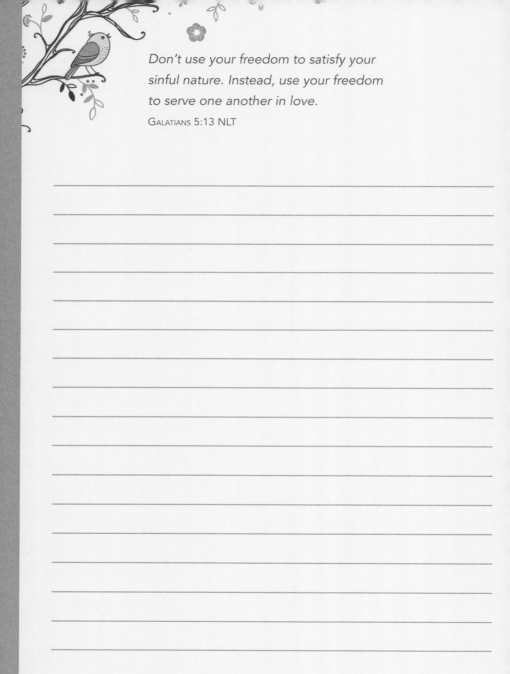

Don't use your freedom to satisfy your sinful nature. Instead, use your freedom to serve one another in love.

GALATIANS 5:13 NLT

_____

_____

_____

_____

_____

_____

_____

_____

_____

_____

_____

_____

_____

_____

_____

_____

_____

_____

_____

_____

_____

When you serve, you are showing love.
Remind yourself of that in the mundane
details of the day, and allow the Lord to fill
you with his joy as you continue to serve
those placed in your care.

You will seek me and find me,
when you seek me with all your heart.

JEREMIAH 29:13 ESV

Don't mistake God's patience for his absence.
His timing is perfect and his presence is constant.
Smile today, knowing you have the very best
Father walking alongside you.

"Remember that I commanded you to be strong and brave. Don't be afraid, because the LORD your God will be with you everywhere you go."

JOSHUA 1:9 NCV

Your strength comes from the Lord of all creation. He put the stars in the sky and breathed life into mankind. Allow that truth to make you brave today.

They should be rich in good works and generous to those in need, always being ready to share with others. By doing this they will be storing up their treasure as a good foundation for the future so that they may experience true life.

1 Timothy 6:18-19 NLT

_____

_____

_____

_____

_____

_____

_____

_____

_____

_____

_____

_____

_____

_____

_____

_____

_____

_____

_____

_____

_____

_____

Be encouraged, God values your role as
a mother. Let him guide you and inspire
you as you invest in your children.

On the glorious splendor of your majesty,
and on your wondrous works, I will meditate.

PSALM 145:5 NRSV

It is amazing what a walk with a friend, or a
run through the woods, can do to our soul.
God created us to need air, sunshine, and the
observation of his incredibly beautiful nature.

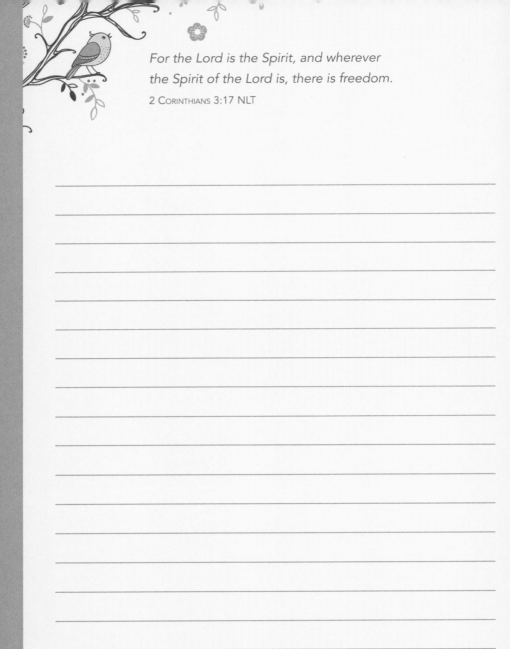

*For the Lord is the Spirit, and wherever
the Spirit of the Lord is, there is freedom.*

2 CORINTHIANS 3:17 NLT

_____

_____

_____

_____

_____

_____

_____

_____

_____

_____

_____

_____

_____

_____

_____

_____

_____

_____

_____

_____

_____

We have a propensity to love rules and regulations,
but many, if not most, of those rules and regulations
God does not require us to keep.

"For I know the plans I have for you," declares the LORD, "plans to prosper you and not to harm you, plans to give you hope and a future."

JEREMIAH 29:11 NIV

_____

_____

_____

_____

_____

_____

_____

_____

_____

_____

_____

_____

_____

_____

_____

_____

_____

_____

_____

_____

Rest in the knowledge that even though you
can't map out a step-by-step plan for your future
or your children's, God's got both covered.

I have learned the secret of being happy at any time in everything that happens, when I have enough to eat and when I go hungry, when I have more than I need and when I do not have enough.

PHILIPPIANS 4:12 NCV

Contentment allows us to see beauty in
situations that are less than ideal. It keeps
us grounded, and it grows a thankful heart.

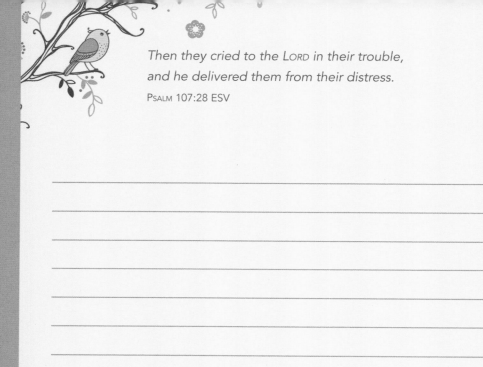

*Then they cried to the L*ORD *in their trouble,*
and he delivered them from their distress.
PSALM 107:28 ESV

_____

_____

_____

_____

_____

_____

_____

_____

_____

_____

_____

_____

_____

_____

_____

_____

_____

_____

_____

_____

_____

_____

_____

_____

_____

_____

_____

_____

_____

_____

_____

_____

_____

_____

_____

_____

_____

_____

_____

We can go boldly to God and he will hear us.
No problem is bigger than he is, and he doesn't
consider our requests insignificant.

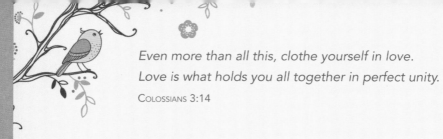

Even more than all this, clothe yourself in love.
Love is what holds you all together in perfect unity.

Colossians 3:14

_____

_____

_____

_____

_____

_____

_____

_____

_____

_____

_____

_____

_____

_____

_____

_____

_____

_____

_____

_____

_____

_____

_____

_____

_____

_____

_____

_____

_____

_____

_____

_____

_____

_____

_____

_____

_____

_____

_____

_____

Not even the cutest boots, most flattering jeans,
or perfect shade of lipstick will make us shine as
brightly as a mom dressed head-to-toe in love.

*"As a mother comforts her child,
so I will comfort you."*

Isaiah 66:13 NIV

_____

_____

_____

_____

_____

_____

_____

_____

_____

_____

_____

_____

_____

_____

_____

_____

_____

_____

_____

_____

_____

_____

_____

_____

_____

_____

_____

_____

_____

_____

_____

_____

_____

_____

_____

_____

_____

_____

_____

_____

_____

_____

_____

Marvel at the gentle power you possess to quiet tears,
banish a nightmare, or reassure after an argument
with a friend. You are a mom: the ultimate place of
safety and comfort for your children.

*"Blessed are those who mourn,
for they shall be comforted."*

MATTHEW 5:4 ESV

_____

_____

_____

_____

_____

_____

_____

_____

_____

_____

_____

_____

_____

_____

_____

_____

_____

_____

_____

When the weight of our loss becomes too
much for us to carry, God carries it for us.

A person's wisdom yields patience;
it is to one's glory to overlook an offense.
PROVERBS 19:11 NIV

It might be easy to beat your children
in an arguing match, but what does that
accomplish? Instead, teach them the art of
answering offense with gentleness and grace.

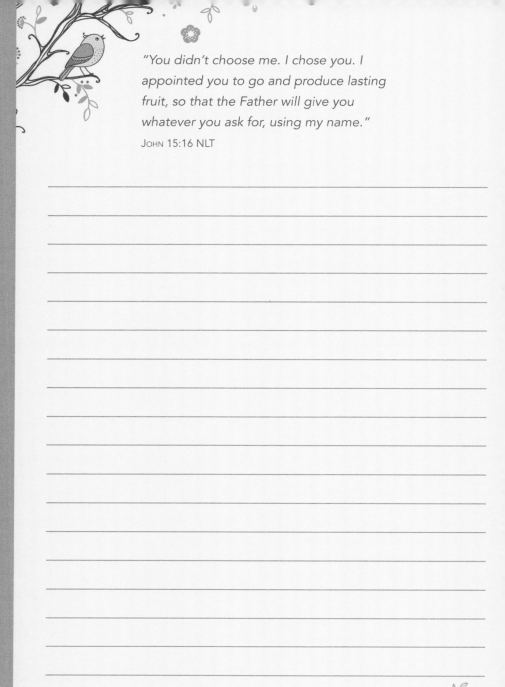

"You didn't choose me. I chose you. I appointed you to go and produce lasting fruit, so that the Father will give you whatever you ask for, using my name."

JOHN 15:16 NLT

Loving our children is as natural as breathing. We really have no choice, do we? Yet we *do* choose them every day as we care for their needs and nurture their hearts.

I call on you, my God, for you will answer me;
turn your ear to me and hear my prayer.
Show me the wonders of your great love.

PSALM 17:6–7 NIV

_____

_____

_____

_____

_____

_____

_____

_____

_____

_____

_____

_____

_____

_____

_____

_____

_____

_____

_____

_____

_____

_____

_____

Don't underestimate the power of an interceding
mother. Even if your children left your home
years ago, God hears your cries.

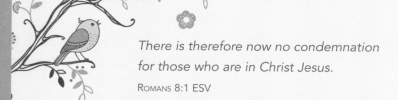

There is therefore now no condemnation for those who are in Christ Jesus.

ROMANS 8:1 ESV

_____

_____

_____

_____

_____

_____

_____

_____

_____

_____

_____

_____

_____

_____

_____

_____

_____

_____

_____

_____

_____

It's by accepting his grace that you can live a victorious life. Let your shame and guilt go today and be free.

*My frame was not hidden from you when I was
made in the secret place, when I was woven
together in the depths of the earth.*

PSALM 139:15 NIV

_____

_____

_____

_____

_____

_____

_____

_____

_____

_____

_____

_____

_____

_____

_____

_____

_____

_____

_____

Parenting can be seen as a long process of
becoming acquainted with our children. What
a gift! They will be both like us and entirely
unique, and we must strive to embrace both.

The Spirit of the Lord will rest on him—
the Spirit of wisdom and understanding.
ISAIAH 11:2 NLT

You don't have to depend on your minimal experience;
you can rely on God's infinite knowledge.

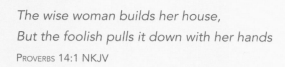

The wise woman builds her house,
But the foolish pulls it down with her hands

PROVERBS 14:1 NKJV

_____

_____

_____

_____

_____

_____

_____

_____

_____

_____

_____

_____

_____

_____

_____

_____

_____

_____

_____

_____

All the mom advice in the world isn't going to stop your children from failing, and it might be more hurtful than helpful sometimes. Instead, be there to pick them up when they do fail, and lovingly teach them how to be successful next time.

The God of all grace, who called you to his eternal glory in Christ, after you have suffered a little while, will himself restore you and make you strong, firm and steadfast.

1 Peter 5:10 NIV

We can take comfort in knowing that when we're in Christ, all suffering is temporary. We may feel crushed, but we are not. God promises to rescue us.

For God so loved the world that he gave his one and only Son, that whoever believes in him shall not perish but have eternal life.

JOHN 3:16 NIV

As a mother, it's easy to imagine darting into traffic, leaping into a raging river, or even sprinting into a burning building to save our children. In light of the sacrifice you'd make for your child, consider the sacrifice that was made for you.